LET'S CELEBRATE YOUR STORY

TIME

CAPSULE

A SERIOUSLY AWESOME JOURNAL

sourcebooks
eXplore

TO NIKLAS AND LINDEN.
THE BOYS WHO REMIND ME TO JUMP,
WIGGLE, GIGGLE, AND PLAY EVERY DAY.

NIKLAS'S ART.
AGE 5

Copyright © 2015, 2020 by Katie Clemons LLC
Cover and internal design © 2020 by Sourcebooks
Cover and internal illustrations by Maryn Arreguín and Katie Clemons LLC (page 2)

Sourcebooks and the colophon are registered trademarks of Sourcebooks.

Published by Sourcebooks eXplore, an imprint of Sourcebooks Kids
P.O. Box 4410, Naperville, Illinois 60567–4410
(630) 961-3900
sourcebookskids.com

Originally published in 2015 in the United States of America by Katie Clemons LLC.

Source of Production: Versa Press, East Peoria, Illinois, USA
Date of Production: October 2019
Run Number: 5016689

Printed and bound in the United States of America.
VP 10 9 8 7 6 5 4 3 2 1

YOUR STORY is a TREASURE

I WOKE UP on a freezing December morning, thrilled to know I had nothing to do. I was halfway through winter break. There was no homework, no alarm clock, and no extracurricular activities to dictate my time. In fact, nothing that morning suggested that my lazy intentions would soon be interrupted by something so awesome.

The furnace kicked on, and I climbed down my bunk bed ladder, just like always. I could hear my brother singing his own rendition of "We Wish You a Merry Christmas" in his bedroom next door. His self-composed lyrics were so annoying! Down the hall, my mom and sister chatted and worked on something in the kitchen. I hoped it was making blueberry muffins from the mix that Mom had purchased.

I loved winter break! It was all so normal—except for the gift our grandparents had mailed. Usually they gave us books and project kits, maybe a gift certificate for a new book or project kit. But not this year.

"Arrr matey!" my sister sing-shouted when I walked into the kitchen. She was wrestling with a fake eye patch wrapped around her head. My brother lumbered in, dropping a pirate hat on me. Eye patches and hats were both presents from our grandparents. They'd also sent fake hook hands, plastic swords, temporary tattoos, at least fifty chocolate coins—half of which we'd already eaten—and a colorful toy parrot I wanted to name Polynesia.

"I wish we had a pirate treasure to hunt," my brother said, flopping into his chair at the table where warm muffins and mugs of milk awaited us.

"You could always make your own treasure chests," Mom suggested as she passed out napkins.

"No we can't," my sister said, trying to snag her hook hand on the edge of the muffin bowl. "We don't have any treasure."

Mom nudged the bowl toward her. "Sure you do. You have your stories."

We all looked at each other.

She smiled. "Instead of a bulky container full of gold, your treasure is words. You can fill your treasure chest with anything you want to save—interesting stories about yourselves, drawings, photographs, or keepsakes. Like that ticket stub from the museum yesterday!"

"That sounds more like a time capsule to me," my brother said.

I was inclined to agree. I was also a bit hesitant—there was no way I wanted to get stuck with a bunch of work over the holiday!

But my mom kept talking about how ordinary people have been assembling time capsules for generations, and the idea started sounding less like a chore and more like something really fun and easy. She said that as we get older, sometimes we forget the everyday details that make up our lives. We don't remember our awesome adventures, achievements, and activities or how they made us feel in the moment. A time capsule is an engaging way to capture anything serious or silly for all time.

I took a few bites of muffin. Then I grinned and said, "I'd like to start making a treasure chest of all our stories today." I wanted to assemble a gift for my future self, something that celebrated this awesome time in my life. I lifted my fist in the air, revealing the temporary tattoo beneath my pajama sleeve, and I looked at my siblings. "Who's with me, mateys?"

My brother slid an eye patch into place and raised his fist. "I'm in!"

My sister lifted her hook hand and said, "Me too!"

Now, my friend, how about you? Are you ready to build an awesome time capsule of your life too? These six guideposts will help you build something fabulous with your *Time Capsule* journal.

❶ Put Pencil to Paper.

Give yourself permission to mark up every page of this journal. Bend the pages. Rip the cover. Accidentally forget it outside overnight. Spill lunch on a page. This book isn't the precious treasure—your stories are. And sometimes the process of recording thoughts gets messy.

Whenever you use this journal, flip to the prompt page that most inspires you and just start writing or doodling. The prompts will guide you to think about your life from different angles. Some pages will make you smile and laugh, while others will challenge you to reflect in unique, memorable ways. You decide what your time capsule becomes as you write, page by page, so don't wait for someday because it'll never come.

If you haven't made a mark in your book yet, start here. Write down any number between 20 and 135:

Now turn to that page and write answers to the questions you see.

❷ WRite WitH authenticity.

A story does not have to be perfect to be valuable. In fact, I've learned that recording some story is infinitely better than writing down none. Don't worry if you don't have all the answers. If a prompt doesn't resonate with you, cross it out and write in your own, or cover it with a photograph or drawing. Use words you always say. Add or alter anything. Ignore any rule you've ever heard about journaling because this book is for *your* story.

Write some journaling rules you've heard that you are NOT going to follow.

1. _____

2. _____

3. _____

❸ COLLECT MEMENTOS.

Keepsakes offer visual excitement to embellish your entries. I always carry a zip pouch with scissors and double-sided tape or glue so I can quickly combine my words with gathered objects such as: a ticket stub, sticker, note from a friend, brochure, postcard, food wrapper, comic, or bumper sticker.

Is there anything you already know you want to include in your journal?

_____

_____

❹ DECORATE AND DOODLE.

This journal is a home for words, but it's also a place to play! These experiments are a few of my favorites. Mark any you'd like to try.

☐ START WITH COLOR.

Think about the questions on the page while you color it in. Use different mediums such as crayons, colored pencils, and watercolors. Then write your thoughts.

☐ CHANGE WRITING UTENSILS.

What would happen if you wrote with something new? Try a paintbrush, your finger dipped in paint, a pine needle covered in mud, a fountain pen, or a highlighter.

☐ WRITE IN DIFFERENT DIRECTIONS.

Rotate the book, then compose sideways or in a circle. Make words go backward or up and down.

☐ CHANGE SCENERY.

If you always journal inside, go outside. Try a dark closet with flashlight, or the sunny corner of someone else's bed. Go where it's noisy or find someplace quiet. Write on the ground. Climb up a tree.

☐ MAKE A CARTOON.

Tell wordless stories through sketches and stick figures or draw speech bubbles.

☐ DIVERSIFY TEXTURE.

Write your answers on a paper bag, piece of packaging, or other interesting paper, then adhere them on the page with glue, double-sided tape, or stickers.

☐ EMBELLISH YOUR PAGE.

Draw arrows, mustaches, zigzags, leafy borders, emojis, or signs.

☐ EMPHASIZE IMPORTANT WORDS AND IDEAS.

Highlight with a marker. Print in all caps or bubble letters. Color in every *o* and *a*. Trace your penmanship with a second color. Write with two pencils pressed together. Draw boxes and underlines.

What other techniques could you play with?

Come join me online for exclusive *Time Capsule* examples from my own diaries, more cool tricks you can try, unexpected strategies for keeping your journal top secret, and journaling jokes that'll crack you up on:

KATIECLEMONS.COM/A/UJ4F

 (OPtiONAL) FiND AN ADULt tO HeLP.

You might be so busy with everyday life that you forget to journal. That's okay! If you'd like, ask an adult to help you…

☐ set aside time to write

☐ discover cool mementos to add to your pages

☐ remember where you put this book

☐ understand new words

☐ recollect important names and information

Who are you asking? Why?

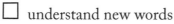

This adult said

☐ yes ☐ no ☐ I'll think about it

⑥ CLAIM THIS JOURNAL.

Look at that! You've already set the tone of your time capsule and started filling it with your ideas. People always say the pen is mightier than the sword; I think you've just proven it. So hang onto that pen or pencil, flip the page, and start assembling the greatest treasure chest of your life. Let's celebrate your story!

♡ Katie

P.S. Want to share your journaling ideas with me? Email **howdy@katieclemons.com** (I answer all my mail) or join me on social media **@katierclemons**, **#katieclemonsjournals**, and **#timecapsulejournal**. And if you're still trying to decide which awesome prompts to answer next, turn to pages 68-69. They're my favorite.

THE PERFECT TREASURE CHEST CONTAINS STORIES CAPTURED FOR ALL TIME

HERE'S A PHOTOGRAPH OR DRAWING OF

ME

HELLO WORLD!

MY FULL NAME IS

_____

I SIGN MY NAME LIKE THIS

_____

I TELL PEOPLE TO CALL ME

_____

I AM _____ YEARS OLD.

TODAY, I START ASSEMBLING THIS TIME CAPSULE!

DATE _____

MY JOURNAL
GUIDELINES

1. IS MY JOURNAL TOP SECRET OR CAN ANYONE ELSE LOOK INSIDE?

2. IF SOMEONE FINDS THIS JOURNAL, THEY SHOULD

☐ EMAIL OR TEXT ME (OR AN ADULT I LIVE WITH) AT

_____

☐ MAIL IT TO MY ADDRESS

_____

_____

☐ COMPLETE IT

☐ DESTROY IT

☐ SHARE PAGES ONLINE #TIMECAPSULEJOURNAL

☐ SELL IT TO A COMIC BOOK PUBLISHER FOR $_____

☐ BURY IT UNDER _____

☐ DONATE IT TO THE _____ MUSEUM

3. DO I HAVE TO ANSWER PROMPTS IN NUMERICAL ORDER? ☐ YES ☐ NO

4. MY TOP FOCUS(ES) IN THIS JOURNAL WILL BE TO

☐ EXPRESS MY THOUGHTS

☐ USE PERFECT GRAMMAR

☐ CAPTURE MEMORIES

☐ RECORD NEW DISCOVERIES

☐ DOCUMENT EVERY NANOSECOND OF MY LIFE

☐ HAVE FUN

☐ _____

5. IS THERE A SPECIFIC DATE WHEN THIS JOURNAL MUST BE COMPLETE?

6. WHAT COULD I DO IF I NEED MORE SPACE TO WRITE?

7. WHAT COULD I DO IF I NEED MORE SPACE TO HOLD MEMENTOS?

8. WILL I WANT TO KEEP ADDITIONAL VOLUMES OF THIS TIME CAPSULE JOURNAL IN THE FUTURE SO I CAN OBSERVE HOW MY LIFE AND STORIES CHANGE?

☐ YES ☐ NO

WHEN?

VOLUME 1: _____

VOLUME 2: _____

VOLUME 3: _____

9. HOW WOULD I LIKE TO CELEBRATE THE COMPLETION OF THIS TIME CAPSULE?

10. ARE THERE OTHER GUIDELINES I'D LIKE TO ESTABLISH BEFORE I DIVE IN?

RIGHT NOW

I'M REALLY EXCITED ABOUT

I'M LESS EXCITED ABOUT

THIS IS ME WHEN I FEEL

OVERJOYED

CRANKY

SLEEPY

INTRIGUED

NERVOUS

PROUD

WORDS THAT DESCRIBE ME

ALWAYS SLEEPING

A MASTER LAUNDRY HOARDER

CAPABLE

LATE FOR DINNER

BOUND FOR SUCCESS

INTELLIGENT

BRAVE

JOYFUL

ALWAYS HUNGRY

COURAGEOUS

A REAL SNUGGLE MACHINE

A TECH GENIUS

ATHLETIC

STRONG

A SKILLED TIME-WASTER

CREATIVE

GROWING FAST

DOWNRIGHT AMAZING

CURIOUS

HAPPY

GENTLE ON MYSELF

HUMBLE

MOTIVATED

FULL OF MUSCLES

FULL OF BRAINS

INSPIRING

PATIENT

KIND

WITTY

ADORABLE

RESOURCEFUL

UNIQUE

Mark the appropriate words

20

FUN TO BE WITH

GIVING

A BRILLIANT GENIUS

OUR FUTURE PRESIDENT

THE GREAT AND POWERFUL

LOVING

A TALENTED DEBATER

WORTHY

A DOER

A DREAMER

GRATEFUL

DEEPLY LOVED

A DAREDEVIL

SILLY

TWO OF MY BEST QUALITIES INCLUDE:

1.

2.

THESE ARE VALUABLE CHARACTER TRAITS BECAUSE

THESE ARE MY FAVORITE BOOKS

IF I WROTE
A BOOK,
THE COVER
WOULD
LOOK LIKE
THIS

MY BOOK WOULD BE ABOUT

DATE

THE MAIN CHARACTERS WOULD BF

THE SFTTING WOULD BE

MY FAVORITE PART OF THE BOOK WOULD BE

MY BOOK
☐ WOULD NOT BE ILLUSTRATED
☐ WOULD BE ILLUSTRATED BY _____.

THE STORY WOULD BE SO _____ THAT
IT'D WIN AN AWARD FOR _____!

PEOPLE COULD GET A COPY OF MY BOOK FOR $_____
AT_____.

I'D ALSO GIVE AWAY _____ FREE COPIES TO

_____.

IT'S GOOD TO BE BORED SOMETIMES BECAUSE THAT'S WHEN I

SOME OF THE COOLEST ADVICE I EVER RECEIVED

①

②

③

④

I'M USUALLY CARRYING

I CAN RECITE EVERY WORD OF

I'M PROUD OF MYSELF FOR

HERE I AM

THE BEST PART OF BEING AGE _____ IS

_____

_____

I HAVE _____ TEETH

I LOVE WEARING THIS TOP BECAUSE

_____

_____

I WEAR
☐ GLASSES
☐ SUNGLASSES
☐ GOGGLES

I SMILE A LOT WHEN

_____

MY PERSONAL THEME SONG COULD BE

_____

_____

I PREFER ☐ SHOWERS ☐ BATHS ☐ STAYING DIRTY

☐ _____

MY HAIR IS USUALLY _____

I ALWAYS SAY " _____ "

I TYPICALLY HAVE ON ☐ JEANS ☐ PANTS ☐ SHORTS

☐ A SKIRT/DRESS ☐ A SWIMSUIT ☐ PAJAMAS ☐ NOTHING!

IT TAKES ME _____ SECONDS TO PUT THESE

_____ ON MY FEET.

MY BODY ENABLES ME TO _____

MY POCKETS OFTEN HOLD _____

MY BELLY IS FULL OF _____

☐ TRUE ☐ FALSE MY KNEES HAVE SCABS, SCRAPES, AND

BRUISES. THAT'S BECAUSE _____

_____

I'M NOT A FAN OF WEARING _____

I LOVE MY BODY JUST HOW IT IS BECAUSE _____

_____

I WONDER WHAT WOULD HAPPEN IF...

HERE'S A MAP OF
EVERYWHERE I'VE BEEN

I'VE ALREADY LIVED IN THESE PLACES

IN THE FUTURE, I IMAGINE MYSELF LIVING IN

I DREAM OF ONE DAY VISITING

HERE'S ME IN MY PAJAMAS

MOST NIGHTS I

- [ ] STAY UP LATE
- [ ] LOSE MY BLANKET
- [ ] LOSE MY PILLOW
- [ ] DREAM
- [ ] SLEEP IN
- [ ] SLEEP LIKE A ROCK
- [ ] SNORE
- [ ] SLEEPWALK
- [ ] TALK IN MY SLEEP

- [ ] GET CHILLY
- [ ] FEEL LIKE I'M ROASTING
- [ ] WAKE UP EARLY
- [ ] BARELY SLEEP
- [ ] WAKE UP CRABBY
- [ ] DROOL
- [ ] GRIND MY TEETH
- [ ] _____
- [ ] _____

HERE'S MY BED

I LIKE TO SLEEP WITH _____

LYING HERE, I HEAR

I GO TO SLEEP AT ___ AND WAKE UP AT ___

I'M MOST AWAKE DURING THE

I'M tracing MY HAND HERE

I'M tracing
MY FOOT HERE

I ESTIMATE THE NUMBER OF

- [ ] STUFFED ANIMALS I OWN

- [ ] DIRTY PAIRS OF UNDERWEAR I HAVE

- [ ] DOLLARS I'VE SAVED

- [ ] FRECKLES OR MOLES ON MY BODY

- [ ] BOOKS IN MY BEDROOM

- [ ] PAIRS OF SHOES I OWN

- [ ] TIMES I'VE SAID "_____!" TODAY

- [ ] TIMES I'VE COMPLAINED "I'M BORED" THIS WEEK

- [ ] _____

- [ ] _____

- [ ] _____

HERE'S A KEEPSAKE
FROM MY LIFE RIGHT NOW

☐ TICKET STUB

☐ QUOTE, POEM, OR LYRIC

☐ RECEIPT

☐ LIST OR NOTE
FROM MY POCKET

☐ PHOTO OR PICTURE

☐ NEWSPAPER CLIPPING

☐ PAPER FROM SCHOOL

☐ _____

HOW to CONViNCE MY faMiLY I NEED aN awesOMe _____ !

❶ _____

_____

❷ _____

_____

❸ _____

_____

❹ _____

_____

SOME OF MY FAVORITE FOODS

SANDWICH

Restaurant Meal

VEGETABLE

Dessert

Pizza

ice cream

Snack

THE MOST HYSTERICAL JOKES OF ALL TIME

WHEN I WAS A LOT YOUNGER, THIS JOKE ALWAYS GOT ME ROLLING.

DON'T REMEMBER? ASK AN OLDER FAMILY MEMBER.

HA-HA!

TOO FUNNY!

IF I HAD A TAIL

IF I HAD WINGS

DATE

A PEEK IN MY BRAIN

THE BEST TIME TO HELP
WITH CHORES IS

I DON'T LIKE TO CLEAN THE

I ALWAYS FORGET

I ALWAYS REMEMBER

ME IN THE MORNING

I WOKE UP BECAUSE _____.

☐ I'M UP AND READY TO ROLL!

☐ WHERE'S MY BED?

☐ I'M SO HUNGRY.

☐ I NEED A CUP OF _____.

☐ NOBODY TALK TO ME.

☐ I'M CURRENTLY SINGING _____.

☐ I HAVE NO IDEA WHAT TO EXPECT TODAY.

☐ I'M GOING TO NEED TIME TODAY TO _____.

I THINK MY DAY WILL BE FULL OF

ME AT NIGHT

I WANT TO / DON'T WANT TO GO TO SLEEP BECAUSE

....

☐ I'M UP AND READY TO KEEP GOING!

☐ WHERE'S MY BED?

☐ I'M SO HUNGRY.

☐ I NEED A CUP OF ....

☐ I'M CURRENTLY READING ....

☐ I'M READY TO DREAM ABOUT ....

☐ MY SLEEP DELAY TACTICS ....

MY DAY WAS FULL OF

....

AROUND HERE

I'M CURRENTLY SITTING ON

MY FEET ARE THE SAME SIZE AS

MY HAIR IS THE COLOR OF

I'M REALLY FAST AT

I'M NOT VERY MOTIVATED TO

THE HIGHEST THING IN THE KITCHEN I CAN REACH IS

THE WEATHER OUTSIDE LOOKS

I'M REALLY GLAD THAT I

I HOPE I NEVER HAVE TO EAT ANOTHER BITE OF

LATER TODAY, I'M GOING TO

IF I WERE A SUPERHERO, I'D WANT EVERYONE TO
CALL ME _____, AND I'D
BE INCREDIBLE AT_____
_____!

Here's a picture of me being
SERIOUSLY AWESOME

FIVE THINGS I CAN'T LIVE WITHOUT

1.
2.
3.
4.
5.

FIVE THINGS I GOT RID OF RECENTLY

1.
2.
3.
4.
5.

FIVE THINGS I'D LIKE TO OWN ONE DAY

1.
2.
3.
4.
5.

I HAVE TO WRITE THIS DOWN BEFORE I FORGET!

I GIVE IT ☆☆☆☆☆ STARS!

I OFTEN WONDER...

HERE'S A PICTURE OF ME
IN MY COMMUNITY

MY COMMUNITY IS SO _____

AND _____ BECAUSE _____

_____ !

54

AROUND HERE, I SPEND A LOT OF TIME

IT'S BEEN A WHILE SINCE I'VE

IF MY COMMUNITY HAD A SOUNDTRACK, IT'D BE CALLED

IT WOULD INCLUDE THESE SONGS

1.

2.

3.

THE COVER WOULD LOOK LIKE THIS

THE VOLUME CONTROL WOULD BE ADJUSTED TO

EVERYONE WOULD EAT _____ WHILE

LISTENING TO IT ☐ INCLUDING ME ☐ BUT NOT ME

I GIVE MY COMMUNITY ☆☆☆☆☆ STARS!

DATE

TODAY'S CHECKLIST

☐ TRY SOMETHING NEW

☐ LAUGH

☐ BE HELPFUL

☐ SAY THANK YOU

☐ EAT A NEW FOOD OR SOMETHING I DON'T NORMALLY LIKE

☐ HAVE FUN

☐ _____

☐ _____

☐ _____

I HOPE THAT ONE DAY I GET THE CHANCE TO

DATE

IF I WERE  BOSS

I'D FILL THE
FRIDGE WITH

1. _____

2. _____

3. _____

4. _____

5. _____

I'D ALWAYS

_____

I'D NEVER

_____

A TYPICAL SCHOOL DAY WOULD LOOK LIKE

_____

THIS IS MY FACE WHEN I FEEL

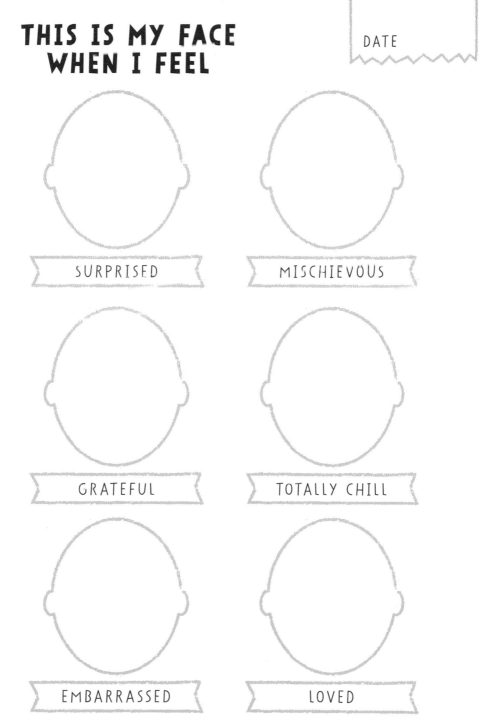

SURPRISED

MISCHIEVOUS

GRATEFUL

TOTALLY CHILL

EMBARRASSED

LOVED

MY NEXT BIRTHDAY IS ON _____

I'LL BE _____ YEARS OLD, WHICH IS

AN AWESOME AGE BECAUSE

I ALWAYS FEEL SPECIAL ON MY BIRTHDAY BECAUSE

MY FAMILY AND I CELEBRATE BY

ONE OF MY MOST TREASURED BIRTHDAY MEMORIES IS

TO ME!

IF I COULD DO ANYTHING ON MY NEXT BIRTHDAY, I'D WANT TO

HERE'S WHAT I'D CHOOSE TO EAT FOR EACH MEAL

BREAKFAST _____

LUNCH _____

DINNER _____

I WOULDN'T NEED TO SPEND ANY TIME ON

THE ULTIMATE
BIRTHDAY CAKE
OF MY DREAMS

THIS FELT
SCARY AT FIRST

I ALMOST DIDN'T DO IT ☐ TRUE ☐ FALSE

HERE'S THE STORY

THE EXPERIENCE MADE ME FEEL _____

THE TOUGHEST PART WAS _____

THE BEST PART WAS _____

IN THE END, IT FELT AWESOME ☐ TRUE ☐ FALSE

I'D DO IT AGAIN ☐ TRUE ☐ FALSE

I'D ENCOURAGE OTHER PEOPLE TO TRY IT
☐ TRUE ☐ FALSE

I GIVE IT ☆☆☆☆☆ STARS!

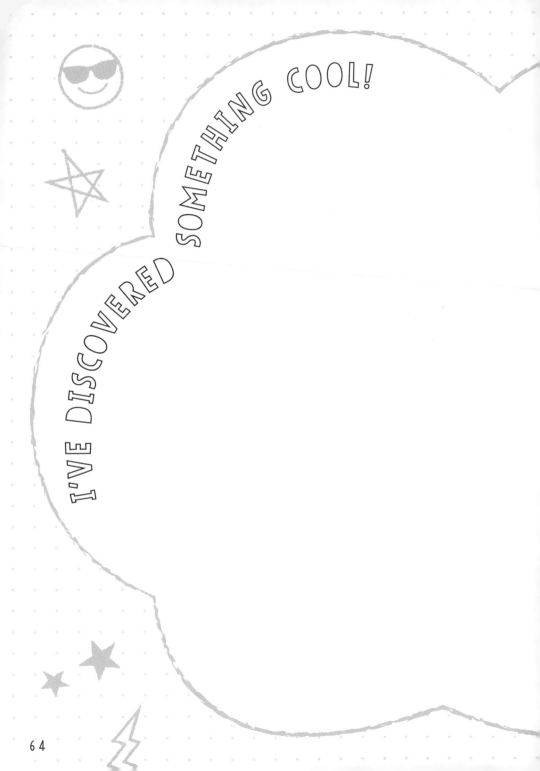

I'VE DISCOVERED SOMETHING COOL!

AROUND HERE I'M SEEING

ABOVE ME

AT EYE LEVEL

BELOW ME

BIGGER THAN ME

SAME SIZE AS ME

SMALLER THAN ME

A BREAKFAST I USUALLY EAT

A LUNCH I TYPICALLY EAT

A DRINK I CONSISTENTLY SWALLOW

A DINNER I OFTEN EAT

THIS IS MY FAMILY

OUR NAMES AND AGES

MY FAMILY IS SERIOUSLY AWESOME BECAUSE

1. _____

2. _____

3. _____

4. _____

5. _____

I APPRECIATE EACH MEMBER BECAUSE

OUR THEME SONG COULD BE

MY FAMILY MAKES ME HAPPY WHEN

I HOPE I BRING THEM HAPPINESS WHEN

I CAN'T WAIT TO _____ WITH THEM

SOON BECAUSE _____

THREE THINGS AROUND HERE

I'M GRATEFUL FOR

1.
2.
3.

I'M CHUCKLING ABOUT

1.
2.
3.

I'M CURRENTLY WORKING ON AND ENJOYING

1.
2.
3.

I'M USING TECHNOLOGY TO

1.
2.
3.

I WANT TO HANG ONTO THIS MEMENTO FROM MY LIFE RIGHT NOW

IT'S A

☐ TICKET STUB

☐ QUOTE, POEM, OR LYRIC

☐ RECEIPT

☐ LIST OR NOTE FROM MY POCKET

☐ PHOTO OR PICTURE

☐ NEWSPAPER CLIPPING

☐ PAPER FROM SCHOOL

☐ _____

I'M ADDING IT TO MY JOURNAL BECAUSE

IF MY LIFE BECAME A MOVIE

IT WOULD BE CALLED _____.

I'D DEDICATE IT TO_____

_____

AND DONATE [SOME/ALL] OF THE PROFITS TO

_____

I'D HAVE _____

PLAY THE PART OF ME BECAUSE _____

_____.

THE AUDIENCE WOULD LOL WHEN _____

_____

THEY'D BE ON THE EDGE OF THEIR SEATS WHEN

_____

I'D MAKE A SECRET GUEST APPEARANCE DURING THE

SCENE WHERE _____

_____

THERE ☐ WOULD ☐ WOULD NOT BE KISSING.

VIEWERS WOULD GIVE IT ☆☆☆☆☆ STARS AND

WATCH IT _____ TIMES AT THE THEATER!

HERE'S THE MOVIE POSTER

THREE OF MY MOST AMAZING ACCOMPLISHMENTS

1

2

3

ANOTHER GOAL I STILL WANT TO ACHIEVE

AWESOME

KIND THINGS I CAN SAY TO MYSELF ON A DIFFICULT DAY

DATE

AROUND HERE, A LOT OF PEOPLE

wear

say

carry

enjoy

go to

_____

AROUND HERE, I

DATE

wear

say

carry

enjoy

go to

I LIKE BEING SIMILAR TO EVERYONE WHEN

I ENJOY BEING UNIQUE WHEN

WONDERFUL THINGS I'VE EXPERIENCED

1

2

3

4

INCREDIBLE THINGS I STILL HOPE TO DO

1

2

3

4

IF I COULD INVENT A HOLIDAY EVERYONE COULD ENJOY

IT WOULD BE A DAY FOR CELEBRATING

_____

- ☐ YIPPEE! NO SCHOOL TODAY.

- ☐ MOST ADULTS DON'T GO TO WORK.

- ☐ GROCERY STORES CLOSE.

- ☐ MY FAMILY GETS TO BE TOGETHER.

- ☐ EVERYONE GOES TO _____.

- ☐ MOST CELEBRATIONS HAPPEN INDOORS/OUTSIDE.

THE DATE ON THE CALENDAR:

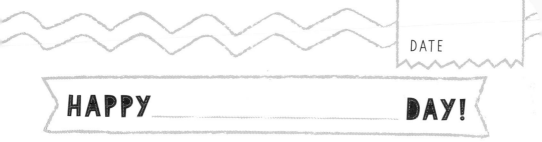

HAPPY _____ DAY!

EVERYONE WOULD EAT

WE'D DECORATF WITH

STORES WOULD BE FILLED WITH

WE'D ALL GIVE EACH OTHER

WE'D ALL SING

I THINK MY FAMILY WOULD ENJOY THIS HOLIDAY
BECAUSE

I THINK IT WOULD MAKE PEOPLE I'VE NEVER MET
HAPPY BECAUSE

MY BEDROOM MAKES ME FEEL

VIEW OUT OF MY WINDOW

THINGS ON MY WALLS

STUFF ON MY FLOOR

EVERYTHING ON MY BED

WHERE I'M SUPPOSED TO PUT MY CLOTHES

WHERE MY CLOTHES ARE NOW

IF I HAD THE HOUSE TO MYSELF, I WOULD

ALL THE WAYS I CAN RECORD MY NAME

IN MY VERY OFFICIAL SIGNATURE

BACKWARDS

IN BLOCK OR BUBBLE LETTERS

AS A DRAWING

LIKE A PIRATE

WITH REALLY TALL LETTERS

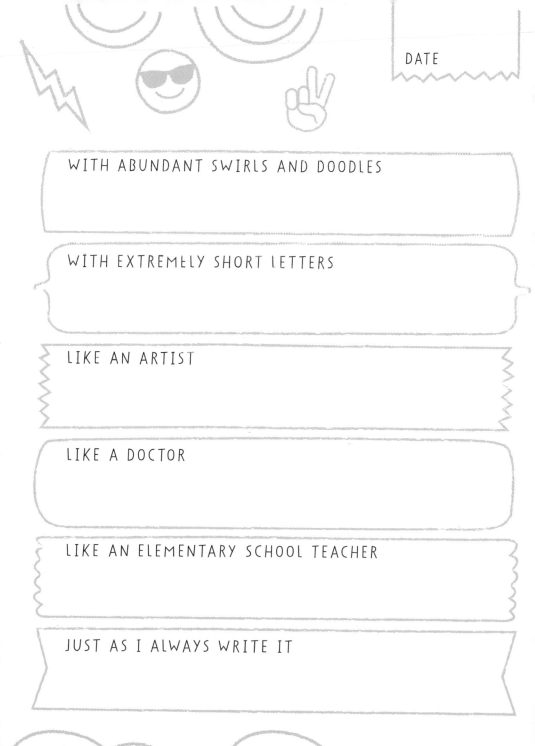

WITH ABUNDANT SWIRLS AND DOODLES

WITH EXTREMELY SHORT LETTERS

LIKE AN ARTIST

LIKE A DOCTOR

LIKE AN ELEMENTARY SCHOOL TEACHER

JUST AS I ALWAYS WRITE IT

I WaNt to LeaRN HOW to

1.

2.

3.

4.

5.

THIS IS THE STORY OF

A TIME I HELPED SOMEONE
WHEN I DIDN'T HAVE TO

ASSISTING THIS PERSON MADE ME FEEL

I THINK IT MADE THAT PERSON FEEL

☐ I'D DO IT AGAIN

SOMEONE I ADMIRE

ADD A PICTURE!

HERE'S PART OF THIS PERSON'S STORY

THE #1 REASON THIS PERSON INSPIRES ME IS

AN INSPIRATIONAL QUOTE BY THIS PERSON

ONE OBSTACLE THIS PERSON HAD TO OVERCOME WAS

I THINK ☐ I WOULD TRY TO DO THAT ☐ I COULDN'T TRY TO DO THAT BECAUSE

I BELIEVE THIS PERSON MAKES OUR COMMUNITY OR WORLD A BETTER PLACE BECAUSE

I THINK I'M A LOT LIKE MY HERO WHEN

I COULD STRIVE TO BE MORE LIKE THIS PERSON BY

DATE

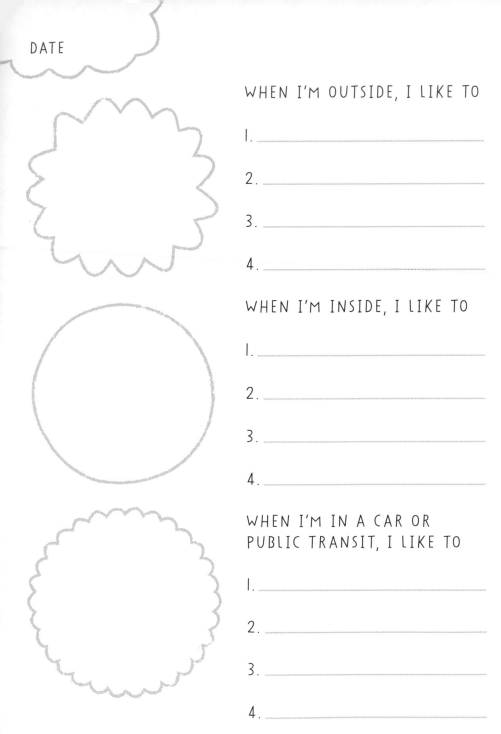

WHEN I'M OUTSIDE, I LIKE TO

1. _____

2. _____

3. _____

4. _____

WHEN I'M INSIDE, I LIKE TO

1. _____

2. _____

3. _____

4. _____

WHEN I'M IN A CAR OR
PUBLIC TRANSIT, I LIKE TO

1. _____

2. _____

3. _____

4. _____

I'M GRATEFUL FOR

this place

this person

this memory

this experience

this stranger's kindness

this club or organization

HERE'S A PICTURE OF ME ENJOYING WINTER

I GIVE WINTER ☆☆☆☆☆ STARS
AT THE BEGINNING OF THE SEASON
AND ☆☆☆☆☆ BY THE END.

THE BEST THINGS TO DO EACH WINTER ARE

1.

2.

3.

THE ANIMAL I'M MOST SIMILAR TO IN WINTER IS

WE ☐ ALWAYS ☐ SOMETIMES ☐ NEVER GET SNOW HERE,
WHICH GENERALLY MAKES ME FEEL

FOR ME, WINTER IS A TIME TO ☐ SNUGGLE UP INSIDE
☐ BUNDLE UP AND GET OUTSIDE BECAUSE

☐ POUR ME ANOTHER MUG OF _____

☐ LET IT SNOW!

☐ SOMEBODY TURN UP THE HEAT.

☐ I HAVEN'T SEEN THE SUN FOR _____ DAYS.

☐ WHEN I GROW UP, I THINK I'D LIKE TO LIVE SOMEWHERE
_____ ER.

☐ OH, IT'S NOT THAT COLD HERE.

☐ I OWN LONG UNDERWEAR.

HERE'S A PICTURE OF ME SAVORING SUMMER

I GIVE SUMMER ☆☆☆☆☆ STARS
AT THE BEGINNING OF THE SEASON
AND ☆☆☆☆☆ BY THE END.

THE BEST THINGS TO DO EACH SUMMER ARE

1.

2.

3.

THE ANIMAL I'M MOST SIMILAR TO IN SUMMER IS

WE ☐ ALWAYS ☐ SOMETIMES ☐ NEVER GET IN THE WATER, WHICH GENERALLY MAKES ME FEEL

FOR ME, SUMMER IS A TIME TO ☐ STAY INSIDE
☐ PUT ON SUNBLOCK AND GET OUTSIDE BECAUSE

☐ OUCH! I GET SUNBURNS.

☐ PASS ME AN ICE COLD _____ TO DRINK.

☐ SOMEBODY TURN UP THE AIR CONDITIONING.

☐ I HAVEN'T SEEN RAIN FOR _____ DAYS.

☐ WHEN I VACATION, I LIKE TO GO SOMEWHERE
_____ ER.

☐ OH, IT'S NOT THAT HOT HERE.

I OWN _____ SWIMSUITS, _____ HATS, & _____ SHORTS.

I'LL BE PROUD OF MYSELF FOR

I'LL BE ABLE TO RECITE EVERY WORD OF

I'LL USUALLY BE CARRYING

HERE I AM

IN _____ YEARS

THE BEST PART OF BEING AGE _____ WILL BE

_____

_____

I'LL HAVE _____ TEETH

I'LL LOVE WEARING THIS TOP BECAUSE

_____

_____

I'LL WEAR
☐ GLASSES
☐ SUNGLASSES
☐ GOGGLES

I'LL SMILE A LOT WHEN

_____

MY PERSONAL THEME SONG COULD BE

_____

I'LL PREFER ☐ SHOWERS ☐ BATHS ☐ STAYING DIRTY

☐ _____

MY HAIR WILL USUALLY_____

I'LL ALWAYS SAY _____

I'LL TYPICALLY HAVE ON ☐ JEANS ☐ PANTS ☐ SHORTS
☐ A SKIRT/DRESS ☐ A SWIMSUIT ☐ PAJAMAS ☐ NOTHING!

IT'LL TAKES ME _____ SECONDS TO PUT

THESE _____ ON MY FEET.

MY BODY WILL ENABLE ME TO _____

MY POCKETS WILL OFTEN HOLD _____

MY BELLY WILL BE FULL OF _____

☐ TRUE ☐ FALSE MY KNEES WILL HAVE SCABS, SCRAPES,

AND BRUISES. THAT'S BECAUSE _____

_____

I WON'T BE A FAN OF WEARING _____

I'LL LOVE MY BODY JUST HOW IT IS BECAUSE _____

_____

IN THE FUTURE, I PREDICT

I WON'T HAVE TO SPEND ANY MORE TIME ON

I'LL HAVE MORE TIME TO

I'LL BE REALLY GREAT AT

MY FAMILY WILL STILL HAVE TO REMIND ME TO

I'LL GO TO BED AT

I'LL WAKE UP AT

I'LL EAT A LOT OF

BUT I WON'T EAT ANY MORE

MARK THE WORDS YOU'D LIKE TO BE!

DEEPLY LOVED	WISE
POPULAR	IMPRESSIVE
STRESSED	PHYSICALLY FIT
FLEXIBLE	APPRECIATED
GRATFFUL	RICH
ROMANTIC	CREATIVE
ADVENTUROUS	CONTENT
KIND	REALLY BUSY
GENEROUS	HELPFUL
FAMOUS	HARDWORKING
HAPPY	ORGANIZED

THE MOST IMPORTANT OF THESE TRAITS WILL BE   BECAUSE

IF MY FUTURE SELF REMEMBERS JUST ONE THING ABOUT MY LIFE TODAY, I HOPE it's

I REMEMBER A STORY OR TWO FROM WHEN I WAS MUCH YOUNGER.

SOMETIMES I WORRY ABOUT THESE THINGS

1.

2.

3.

THEY BOTHER ME BECAUSE

MAYBE I COULD EASE MY CONCERNS BY

OLDER PEOPLE WHO MIGHT BE ABLE TO HELP ME INCLUDE

TWO THINGS FROM
THIS PAST WEEK

THINGS I FORGOT TO DO

1.

2.

WAYS OTHER PEOPLE MADE ME HAPPY

1.

2.

WAYS I HOPE I BROUGHT OTHER PEOPLE JOY

1.

2.

THINGS I'M GRATEFUL THAT HAPPENED

1.

2.

MOMENTS THAT MADE ME LAUGH OR SMILE

1.

2.

JOBS I'D LIKE TO TRY SOME DAY

1.

2.

3.

PEOPLE I'D LIKE TO MEET ONE DAY

1.

2.

3.

MILESTONES AND ACHIEVEMENTS I'D LIKE TO EXPERIENCE ONE DAY

1.

2.

3.

ONE OF THE BEST PRESENTS I EVER RECEIVED

FROM: _____

ONE OF THE BEST PRESENTS I EVER GAVE

TO: _____

HERE'S A LIST OF THINGS I'M GLAD I CAN DO

AND HERE'S ONE THING I HAVEN'T BEEN ABLE TO DO...YET!

RIGHT NOW,
MY BEDROOM LOOKS LIKE

- [ ] A TORNADO HIT
- [ ] A TORNADO NEEDS TO HIT
- [ ] A CLEANING COMMERCIAL
- [ ] A HISTORIC SITE
- [ ] A GOLD MINE
- [ ] A SCIENCE EXPERIMENT
- [ ] A TOY STORE
- [ ] _____

HERE'S a PicTURE

HOW I CLEAN MY ROOM
IN _____ MINUTES

1.

2.

3.

4.

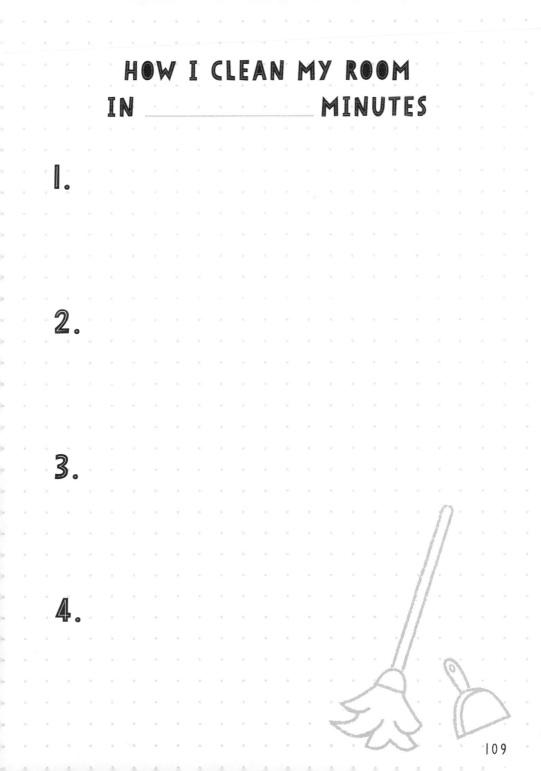

DATE

ENCOURAGING WORDS AND COMPLIMENTS PEOPLE HAVE GIVEN ME

THIS IS THE STORY OF
RECENTLY SPENDING TIME
WITH SOMEONE I LOVE

A GOOD FRIEND

IS SOMEONE WHO

I THINK _____ IS A GREAT FRIEND BECAUSE

1.

2.

3.

WE'VE KNOWN EACH OTHER SINCE

WHEN WE'RE TOGETHER, WE ENJOY

WHEN WE'RE NOT TOGETHER, WE COMMUNICATE BY

I TRY TO BE A GOOD FRIEND BY

HeRe's a PiCtuRe Of tHe twO Of uS BeiNG

_____

&

_____ _____

BRAVERY

I FEEL BRAVE WHEN

I FEEL NERVOUS OR UNCOMFORTABLE WHEN

I REMEMBER A TIME WHEN I DECIDED TO DO
SOMETHING COURAGEOUS EVEN THOUGH I FELT
NERVOUS. HERE'S THE STORY

I THINK IT CAN BE IMPORTANT FOR ME TO TAKE
ACTION EVEN WHEN I'M FEELING UNCERTAIN
BECAUSE

Here's a picture
OF ME BEING COURAGEOUS

THREE THINGS...

...I always have time for

1.
2.
3.

...I never have time for

1.
2.
3.

...I struggle with

1.
2.
3.

...I'm naturally good at

1.
2.
3.

MY TYPICAL WEEKDAY

6:00

7:00

8:00

9:00

10:00

11:00

NOON

1:00

2:00

3:00

4:00

5:00

6:00

7:00

8:00

9:00

10:00

I LIKE TO

TASTE

FEEL

WATCH

SMELL

BEGIN

RELAX WITH

FINISH

GO TO

TRY

REMEMBER

WEAR

HEAR

I DON'T LIKE TO

TASTE

FEEL

WATCH

SMELL

BEGIN

RELAX WITH

FINISH

GO TO

TRY

REMEMBER

WEAR

HEAR

ONE DAY, I'D LIKE TO

TASTE

FEEL

WATCH

SMELL

BEGIN

RELAX WITH

FINISH

GO TO

TRY

REMEMBER

WEAR

HEAR

THREE THINGS...

...I SEE WHEN I LOOK IN THE MIRROR

1.
2.
3.

...I NOTICE WHEN I OPEN THE FRONT DOOR

1.
2.
3.

...I TRY TO DO FOR THE ENVIRONMENT

1.
2.
3.

...I HOPE NEVER CHANGE ABOUT ME

1.
2.
3.

HERE'S A PICTURE
OF MY HOME

I'VE LIVED HERE SINCE _____.

MY HOME HAS _____ BEDROOMS,

_____ BATHROOMS, AND A LOT OF

_____.

I LOVE THIS PLACE BECAUSE

1.

2.

3.

4.

5.

HERE'S WHERE I

Eat	Relax	Journal	

I CHERISH THIS MEMORY

MY HOME GETS ☆☆☆☆☆ STARS FROM ME!

THIS IS THE STORY OF

A TIME I TAUGHT SOMEONE HOW TO DO
SOMETHING I ALREADY UNDERSTOOD

HELPING THIS PERSON MADE ME FEEL

I THINK GAINING THIS KNOWLEDGE FROM ME MADE
THAT PERSON FEEL

☐ I'D DO IT AGAIN

AROUND HERE

I ALWAYS RIDE

☐ MY BIKE

☐ THE BUS

☐ PUBLIC TRANSPORTATION

☐ _____

☐ _____

I ALWAYS CARRY

I DON'T DO MY HOMEWORK UNTIL

IF I COULD SPEND $100 ON ANYTHING RIGHT NOW,
I'D GET

IF I COULD GIVE $100 RIGHT NOW, I'D DONATE IT TO

HERE'S SOMETHING I WON!

I GIVE THE EXPERIENCE
☆☆☆☆☆ STARS!

HERE'S THE STORY

DATE

I HAD TO WORK REALLY HARD AT

WHEN I WON, I REMEMBER FEELING

I KNEW MY FAMILY WAS REALLY PROUD BECAUSE

127

If I were the family cook

Four ways I can make the world a better place

1.

2.

3.

4.

HOW to Have tHe BEST DaY eveR

1.

2.

3.

4.

HOW to fiX tHe WORST DaY eveR

1.

2.

3.

4.

I REMEMBER WHEN

TAUGHT ME HOW TO

AROUND HERE

DATE

I'M REALLY HAPPY THAT

I'M WONDERING WHEN

I'M HOPING I CAN

I WANT TO LEARN ABOUT

PEOPLE I KNOW

THE HAPPIEST

_____

_____

THE MOST HELPFUL

_____

_____

THE HARDEST WORKING

_____

_____

THE FUNNIEST

_____

_____

THE MOST COURAGEOUS

THE MOST GENEROUS

THE MOST PATIENT

THE MOST EMPATHETIC

LOOKING BACK
AT ALL THESE PEOPLE

I REALLY ADMIRE HOW _____ TAKES
TIME TO

I THINK THAT _____ IS REALLY MAKING
A DIFFERENCE IN OUR WORLD BY

_____ PROVES THAT A PERSON CAN BE

I APPRECIATE HOW _____ SEEMS SO
WILLING TO

I THINK I COULD LEARN A LOT FROM _____
BECAUSE

HERE'S A MAP OF MY NEIGHBORHOOD

X MARKS THE SPOT WITH MY HOUSE.

MY NEIGHBORHOOD HAS A LOT OF _____

WHEN I CLOSE MY EYES,

I CAN HEAR _____

I CAN SMELL _____

I CAN FEEL _____

I LOVE LIVING HERE BECAUSE

1.

2.

3.

THIS NEIGHBORHOOD GETS ☆☆☆☆☆ STARS!

THINGS I'M CREATING RIGHT NOW

FiLL-iN-tHe-BLanKs
IN MY BRAIN

I DON'T WANT TO FORGET TO

IF I HAD TO EAT ONE THING FOR
THE REST OF MY LIFE

I WOULD LOVE TO EXPLORE A

I DON'T LIKE GETTING TICKLED ON THE

I DANCE LIKE A

SOME OF MY
FAVORITE THINGS

APP OR WEBSITE

PHRASE I SAY WHEN I'M HAPPY

COLOR

BAND OR MUSICIAN

INSECT

ANIMAL

TEAM OR ATHLETE

BOOK

MOVIE

HOLIDAY TRADITIONS
I LOOK FORWARD TO

THE END. ALMOST.

WHILE I'VE BEEN KEEPING THIS JOURNAL, I LEARNED

NEXT YEAR, I WANT TO LEARN

HERE'S WHAT I ENJOYED ABOUT KEEPING THIS JOURNAL

MY FAVORITE MEMORY RECORDED IN THESE PAGES IS

IF ANYONE EVER ASKS ME FOR ADVICE ON HOW TO KEEP A FABULOUS JOURNAL, I'LL SAY

THat's it.

☐ WAIT! I NEED TO ADD A FEW MORE THINGS:

☐ OKAY. I'M ALL DONE.

WHEN YOUR JOURNAL IS FINISHED, CUT
OUT THIS PAGE AND THE NEXT. PUT YOUR
JOURNAL IN AN ENVELOPE AND SEAL IT
SHUT. TAPE OR GLUE THIS PAGE ON THE
OUTSIDE. THEN HIDE YOUR JOURNAL AND
USE THE NEXT PAGE TO DRAW A MAP.

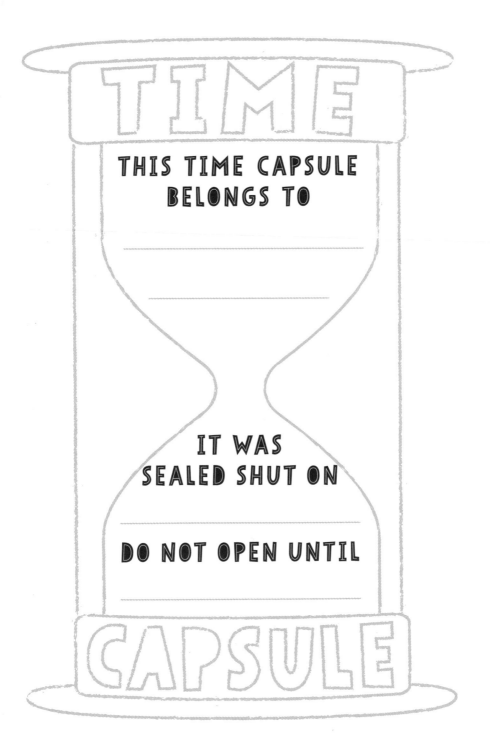